The Adventures of Black Beauty

The Adventures of Black Beauty

MARK TYLER

With 25 full colour illustrations

A Piccolo Original

PAN BOOKS LTD
LONDON

First published 1972 by Pan Books Ltd,
33 Tothill Street, London, SW1.

ISBN 0 330 23518 4

Based on the television series
'The Adventures of Black Beauty'

Printed in Great Britain by
Cox & Wyman Ltd, London, Reading and Fakenham

The stories in this book are based on the London Weekend Television series inspired by Anna Sewell's immortal book and devised by Anthony Gruner and Ted Willis. They are adapted from original screen-plays by Ted Willis, Richard Carpenter, David Butler and Lindsay Galloway.

The actors featured are:

Vicky Gordon	Judi Bowker
Kevin Gordon	Roderick Shaw
Dr Gordon	William Lucas
Amy	Charlotte Mitchell

THE FUGITIVE

Vicky didn't even wait to look at their new home. It was enough that the field stretched almost as far as the eye could see. A vast new world to explore, so different from the crowded, smelly streets of London.

Even now in Victorian England, the Industrial Revolution had turned London into a great sprawling city, the biggest the world had ever known. Vicky hated the hard pavements and the rude, impersonal crowds that jostled you in the streets.

She had nagged and nagged her father to move to the countryside. Now at last they were here.

Her eyes could hardly take it all in. The little thatched cottage with roses around the door, a small yard, a stable, a cluster of trees, a pond, perhaps with fish, and, yes, there to the east on the ridge, what looked like a great forest, though in truth it was only a rather small wood.

The excitement was too much. "Come on!" she cried to her brother Kevin, still dozing after the long journey, his head propped up against a trunk at the back of the wagon.

"I'll race you," she called, "I'll race you to the wood!"

Brother and sister ran across the grass. Back at the wagon lifting off the heavy cases Dr. Gordon smiled. Twins, he thought, were there ever twins so different? They neither looked nor behaved alike.

Kevin the steady one, slow but reliable and Vicky a regular harum-scarum, full of warmth and wild enthusiasm. It made you breathless just trying to keep up with her.

How like her mother. The doctor's face clouded with the memory, and he felt quite alone. But there was no time now for old sorrows. The wagoner had dumped the pile of luggage on the path and Amy Winthrop was telling the man in that bossy way of hers, "Don't you forget now. I want you to tell everyone that Dr. James Gordon M.D. is now in practice at York Cottage."

The man smiled through a gap in his teeth. "Oi'll tell 'em missus, but it won't do no good, will it?" His country accent was thick and he smelt of old cider.

"Why not?" retorted Amy. She didn't like being contradicted.

"You be foreigners from London," he said simply,

as if that were reason enough. He cracked his whip and the old wagon clattered away down the lane.

"What did I tell you," Amy said to the doctor, a note of triumph in her voice. She loved the city and the feel of people round her and the bright, gaslit shops. This place was a wilderness, empty and unfriendly.

"To think we left London for this. No streets, no shops, no people . . ."

"No fogs?" chuckled the doctor.

Amy Winthrop pretended not to listen. In the twelve years she had been with the Gordon family, ever since the children were born, she had learned the habit of listening to only what she wanted to hear.

"Nothing but trees and fields and animals. Ugh!" She shuddered with the thought. Then looking towards the east, where the two children were but specks on the horizon she said, "It's your children I feel sorry for doctor."

Amy need not have worried. The children were happy. They had reached the wood, Vicky darting in and out of the trees, Kevin in pursuit.

Suddenly they heard something. A long, low whine. Almost human, obviously in distress.

Kevin stumbled over a fallen branch he, was still breathless from the run.

"Be quiet," said Vicky crossly. There was the noise again. It came from their right. The two of them picked their way carefully towards it.

Then they saw him.

The riderless horse was jet black except for a white star on his forehead. Great weals tore across his flanks. His reins had tangled up in a thicket. He was trapped and there was fear in his eyes.

"What shall we do?" asked Kevin a little nervously. But already Vicky was freeing the reins and stroking the horse down his nose.

The horse stumbled awkwardly out of the thicket. He walked only on three legs, the other foot held up from the ground, bruised and injured. Vicky whispered softly to the frightened animal and gently he nuzzled against her arm.

"Oh my poor love," she said, "don't worry we won't hurt you."

Afterwards Vicky insisted the horse had smiled and kissed her back. But as Kevin remarked sceptically, he merely looked like a very sick horse indeed.

As the doctor said, animals were different. He knew how to cure people. He could prescribe medicine for whooping cough and measles. But horses. That was something else.

Vicky and Kevin ran the full half mile to the village to find a vet. They were directed to the cottage of an old lady who looked after stray cats, but no, not horses. Old Ebenezer Allingham the village Vet was dead and buried these two years past. There was a young fellow at Crowley, but that was 15 miles or more away.

The two youngsters returned dispirited to York Cottage. Surely the doctor could cure the black horse. Even Amy, fighting off her natural fear of all dumb creatures to bring a bowl of oats to the stable door, declared that horses and humans were all God's creation and that all they needed was a little warmth and lots of love.

That evening at supper, their first meal in their new home, Vicky slipped in a prayer at the end of Grace asking that the black horse would soon get well. The doctor said he was sure the prayer would be answered, but there was no conviction in his voice.

He had spent most of the afternoon in the stable tending the sick animal, Vicky by his side the devoted nurse. Even Kevin hadn't complained when he was asked to clear out the hay, while Amy kept arriving with a continuous supply of hot sweet tea.

The doctor feared the horse would die. If anything, the sickness had grown worse since they had brought the horse down from the wood to the stable. Even if he recovered he would have to be returned to the rightful owner, whoever that might be.

But that was a prospect the doctor thought it best to keep to himself, at least for now.

It was the children's favourite meal: boiled beef and carrots and juicy dumplings. But Amy need not have bothered. Kevin just picked at his meal, while Vicky did not so much as look at her plate.

At last Vicky could stand it no more. She rose from the table, and ran through the door, across the yard to the stable. Kevin started to follow, but his father placed a firm hand on his arm. "Leave her alone, just for a moment," he said gently.

Then suddenly from out of the darkness came a sharp, shrill sound. It was Vicky. And she was screaming.

Two men had stepped out of the shadows of the stable. One medium sized and nondescript, the other tall with a hard face and jutting chin. No wonder Vicky had been scared.

The tall man, whose name was Samson, said with a menace in his voice, "So you are the horse thieves are you?"

The very sound of the hard cruel voice seemed to make the black horse shudder. It was a voice the horse had evidently learnt to know, and to fear.

Dr. Gordon invited the two men into the kitchen and explained how the children had first found the horse and the dreadful condition it had been in.

"We have been looking for that horse all day," said Samson. "He is a runaway and I am taking him back with me this very instant."

It was not often that Dr. Gordon lost his temper. "That is a very ill and frightened animal," he said angrily. "I am a doctor and that animal is in no condition to be moved."

"A horse doctor?" said Samson sarcastically. "That's my uncle's horse. He wants him back and I'm taking him back."

The doctor decided to try sweet reason. "We've no wish to keep your horse, sir," he began, when Vicky who had been eavesdropping from behind the door burst in.

"But we do Daddy, we do want to keep him."

Dr. Gordon ignored the interruption. "Bring your uncle here," he told the man, "bring him in the morning, perhaps the horse will be better then."

True enough by the morning the black horse looked considerably better. There was a sleekness about the coat and brightness in the eye.

Perhaps it had something to do with Vicky's prayer at supper time or perhaps it was because she had spent the entire night in the stable, gently caressing the sick animal's head.

Amy said it was a miracle and the doctor didn't disagree. They were all feeling very pleased with themselves when the clatter of a horse and cart outside brought them back to reality.

It was Samson with a much older man, strapped into a wheelchair. The chair was lowered to the ground. "This is my uncle, Mr. Ryder," said Samson.

Mr. Ryder looked at Amy. "Are you the doctor's wife?" he demanded. Amy blushed and Dr. Gordon quickly explained that his wife had died.

"Widower, eh?" said Mr. Ryder, his voice softening and he added slowly, "I know what that's like."

He seemed to reflect on his words for a few moments, then taking a small silver box from his waistcoat he took out a white pill and swallowed it.

"What are they?" asked the doctor.

"For my heart," said Mr. Ryder, "the old dicky

ticker." He grinned, but there was little humour in the smile.

"Come on," he said impatiently. "Where's the beast. That's what I am here for. Let's take him away."

Vicky burst into sobs.

"What's the matter with her?" asked Mr. Ryder.

"My daughter," explained the doctor, "she found the horse and they have become very attached."

Amy grabbed the doctor's sleeve and whispered in his ear. He thought for a moment and said, "My housekeeper has quite rightly pointed out that as a doctor I could do with a horse to take me around the villages. I wonder, er, is the horse for sale? Perhaps we might . . ."

Vicky's eyes lit up. She stopped sobbing.

"Well," said Mr. Ryder, "I was going to sell it. Yes you can have it. He is a thoroughbred you know. The price is only fifty guineas."

Fifty guineas! It might as well have been fifty thousand, for all the money the Gordons had. Vicky began sobbing again. Mr. Ryder shifted uneasily in his wheelchair. He could not abide the sight or sound of sobbing women.

"Look here," he said, "the horse fair is not until next week. I can't sell the beast till then, if you want to, you can keep him the weekend. I'll be back on Monday."

It was a glorious weekend. The black horse had now quite recovered and Kevin and Vicky took it in turns to ride him.

"Oh, how I wish we weren't so poor!" exclaimed Vicky.

"We might as well wish for the moon," said Kevin glumly.

It was on Sunday, just before supper, that Samson returned again. Kevin met him at the gate.

"You can't take the horse," said Kevin in a panic. "It's not Monday. Mr. Ryder promised, not until Monday."

But Samson was in an even greater panic. "Where's the doctor," he demanded. "It's my uncle. Something terrible."

Dr. Gordon went off with Samson. He returned to the cottage very late that night.

Mr. Ryder did not turn up as promised on Monday. Nor the following Monday, although Samson called frequently, every other day or so, picking up the doctor and returning him, sometimes in the early hours of the morning.

It was another two weeks before Mr. Ryder eventually arrived at York Cottage. This time he didn't have a wheelchair. He jumped down from the cart with the ease of a young man. He was sprightly, and smiling.

"I don't know what you've done Gordon?" he said to the doctor, "but I'm a new man, never felt better. I'm greatly in your debt sir."

He looked over to the two children who, on Amy's orders, were reluctantly preparing the black horse for his journey.

"I've been thinking," continued Mr. Ryder, "about your fee. Perhaps you will agree to a little barter. Will you accept that black beast with my compliments?"

The children were delighted. Even Amy was pleased, and Dr. Gordon announced that they must find a name for this new member of the family.

"What about Jet?" he suggested, "or Swift?"

No, said Vicky, no not Blackbird either, which was Kevin's suggestion, or Lightning which came from Amy.

"We must have something that describes him," said Vicky. "He is black and he is certainly very beautiful.

"Yes, that's it. That's his name – Black Beauty!"

And so they all agreed.

MANTRAP

Vicky woke early, knowing it was a perfect day, before she so much as opened an eye. She could smell honeysuckle, and the rich perfume of earth and grass and dew meeting sun again after the darkness.

Something boomed like a drum outside. Vicky sat bolt upright, as if pulled by an invisible string. Black Beauty, down in the stable, had stamped impatiently.

The sound was not repeated, and as Vicky pattered barefoot to the big china bowl and jug on the washstand, she giggled to herself. "Clever Beauty," she whispered.

There was such a bond of love and admiration between child and horse that Vicky felt sure Black Beauty was anxious to see her. Yet one stamp was enough, and he knew it. Too many "Hurry up and come downstairs" signals would rouse the rest of the household at least an hour before they were ready.

Face glowing from cold water, hair brushed, after a

fashion, Vicky rushed through the daily ordeal of dressing. So many clothes, even in the summer! So many hooks-and-eyes and buttons and tapes!

Opening the front door was hard work. Heavy bolts, top and bottom, a fat iron key fit for the Tower of London, then a chain to juggle loose from its hook. Amy had a terrible fear of being "out in the wilds at the mercy of burglars and gypsies and madmen and convicts and . . ." The list was endless.

A quarter of an hour later, Vicky was riding Black Beauty around the paddock. For a while she was content to circle slowly, glorying in the way the slightest pressure of her foot or dip of the reins was answered by a turn to left or right.

"I can tell you things, you know," she said. Black Beauty nodded, and Vicky laughed in delight. Perhaps he would have nodded anyway, at that moment – Kevin was bound to say so, of course – but she knew better.

Glancing back, she saw the first wisp of smoke from the kitchen chimney. Amy must be coaxing the range back to life. And there was Kevin, clinging to the five-bar gate by the cottage.

"He isn't bad, considering he's a mere boy," she told Black Beauty. The horse whinnied agreement. Knowing she was being watched, she turned towards the far hedge.

Black Beauty took the hint. His stride lengthened, hoofbeats thudding faster. Trees flicked past the corner of Vicky's eye, blurring a little, as her mount headed for an exact target.

A froth of creamy white showed where a thorn bush stood a good three feet lower than the rest of the hedge. Black Beauty gathered himself, Vicky gasped as they left the ground in a wonderful burst of power.

Just like flying, she thought for the thousandth time. Up and over, with a clean impact as Black Beauty, cat-sure on his feet, landed on the far side of the hedge.

"Lovely," Vicky cried. Black Beauty cocked an ear, put his head on one side. Like a grown-up, the shy sort, saying, "Oh, that was nothing, my dear," when giving a Christmas present.

So far, so very good. Cantering through woodland, along a wide strip of rabbit-nibbled turf, Vicky was riding the best horse in the world. She wasn't at all sure that she wasn't the best rider in . . . well, Five Oaks, anyway.

Soon the trees, thinning out, showed inviting mazes of paths. Gentle work with the reins made the horse slow from gallop to canter to an easy walk. "Lets get lost," Vicky said, knowing they would do nothing of the kind, so close to York Cottage.

Suddenly her nose banged into the scratchy depth

of mane. Black Beauty had stopped, without warning. She urged him forward, but this time, he reared.

Vicky slipped out of the saddle and started to walk ahead, reins over one shoulder. "Silly boy, there's nothing there. Come on, it's all right."

Black Beauty came alongside, nudging at her. Absently, she pushed his head away. Now his head swung harder, effortlessly his shoulder barged her aside.

Vicky found herself sitting on the turf. Though she still held the reins, Black Beauty was in charge. Forelegs spread, blocking the path, his eyes held an almost human expression – warning, and fear.

Vicky shivered, half-remembering old fireside tales of ghosts and goblins which frightened animals while human beings were unable to see the danger.

Scrambling to her feet, she froze. The danger wasn't invisible, simply cunningly hidden.

Two wicked lengths of saw-toothed steel lay among the tender green fonds of young bracken, and the tussocky grass. A trap, three feet wide, its jaws forced open against vicious springs. Step inside, trip the springs . . .

"Thank you, Black Beauty, thank you." Shuddering, Vicky remounted and urged the horse back along the path. As soon as they were on open ground, she urged him to a gallop. Angry and frightened by their narrow escape, she wanted to see her father. He would know the best way to fight the trap.

Later that day, Dr. James Gordon started the fight. By paying a visit to Ted Hewitt, Lord Eddington's new gamekeeper. Hewitt and his wife Beth – who happened to be expecting a baby within a few weeks – lived in a rather gloomy, dull red brick cottage at the fringe of the woodland.

Hewitt had been setting the traps all right. Dr. Gordon knew it, as soon as Vicky came flying into the stableyard at York Cottage, pouring out her news and begging him to see the hidden, horrible machine which only Black Beauty had been clever enough to see.

James Gordon, doctor of medicine, served animals as well as human beings. He had only just finished tending a local poacher's collie dog, when Vicky exploded on the scene. The collie's front leg was fearfully injured, obviously by a steel trap. Dr. Gordon, helped by Kevin, had put a splint on the leg but feared that the dog would be lucky to walk again, let alone run after other people's pheasants.

Now, staring into the big shed at the back of the keeper's cottage, Dr. Gordon was angry. The space was full of traps of different kinds, and bundles of wire and twine snares. Gamekeeper Hewitt was defiant. "There's a lot of valuable game on this estate. It's my job to protect it."

Saying nothing, Dr. Gordon stepped past him and dragged a trap from the shelf. It fell with a clang, almost crushing Hewitt's toes, so that he had to jump aside. "I won't have these in the district," Dr. Gordon rapped out. "They are against the law. If I find any more, I'll report you."

He had already been taken by Vicky to the mantrap in the woods, and set it off by poking at it with a branch. The piece of wood was thick, but the steel teeth had crashed through the timber as easily as cheese. God help the man who stepped into it . . . or the child. "Look here, man," said Dr. Gordon, "what if one of my children – *any* child – stumbled into one of these things?"

Hewitt, maybe because he was soon to have a child of his own, nodded slowly. "All right, the mantraps go," he grunted. All the same, he'd heard of this doctor fellow, tending animals for nothing, soft as butter. Him, and his horse-mad brat of a daughter.

"But all the other traps stay," Hewitt warned. "Animals must work, or be eaten. The rest is vermin, to be put down." Dr. Gordon's eyes narrowed, and Hewitt had a flash of fear. This chap wasn't too soft, after all.

"Tell your family to stick to the gallops and the bridle paths, they'll be safe enough," Hewitt added, hastily. He was in an awkward position. Dr. Gordon was a friend of the man who owned this estate, Lord Eddington. Also, he would be looking after Hewitt's wife when she had the baby.

Still, the gamekeeper decided, he just had to keep this job. He had been out of work for three years. And the best, the easiest way of showing results was to cover the ground with traps. If Dr. Gordon didn't like that, it was just too bad.

The doctor realized he would never persuade Hewitt to stop setting traps, cruel things of torture as they were. He shrugged and walked out of the shed. "Your wife – I'd better examine her," was all he said, and Ted Hewitt mumbled his thanks.

That was the start of *The Trapping Summer*. Within days, matters went from bad to worse, with Vicky and her Black Beauty barred from every inch of the Eddington estate.

She should have listened to her father. Dr. Gordon told her that Mrs. Hewitt had a weak heart. The birth of the baby would be a terrible strain on her. "So Hewitt *has* to make good at his job," James Gordon explained. "He's fighting for his wife, and his baby, as well as himself. We'll have to work on him gradually, about the traps. Make him see reason. The more you fight a man like Ted Hewitt, the harder he fights back."

Dr. Gordon smiled at his own words. "That's the curse and blessing of the British nation, sweetheart. The reason we lose battles but win wars; why we're set fair to creating the greatest Empire in history."

Vicky wasn't interested. Oh, she liked Beth Hewitt, but as for "gradually" and "make him see reason" – "Fiddlesticks!" said Vicky Gordon, to herself. She had declared war on Ted Hewitt.

Being allowed on the Eddington estate gallops and bridle paths, Vicky made it a point to check up on the gamekeeper. Soon she found that he was selling pheasants he had shot, rabbits he had trapped. But the game belonged to Lord Eddington, so Hewitt must be stealing. Off to jail with him, then, and hooray for the end of the traps!

Not a bit of it. Hewitt was allowed to sell certain things, Lord Eddington – or rather, his agent – knew all about it, thank you. Vicky tried again, went too far, and was caught.

Hewitt, no fool, found that she was shadowing him. "You're trying to make trouble, interfering all the time," he shouted. "Now you're barred from this estate. If you can't stick to the paths I gave you, out you go. And keep out, young lady!"

The ban was hard enough on Vicky, but her heart seemed to twist when she saw Black Beauty eyeing the broad green acres and tempting woodland of the Eddington estate, over the paddock hedge.

She got no sympathy from her father. If anything, he was . . . not quite angry, but disappointed in her. That made Vicky go cold.

"Remember," he said gently. "The more you fight the Hewitts, the harder they fight back. But worse still, is the effect they have on people who fight them. You, for example."

Vicky's eyes widened in surprise. She was the champion of helpless animals, the fighter against traps!

"Yes, you. Spying on Hewitt, and then thinking the worst when he makes a few honest shillings for his sick wife. That's not like you."

She tried to deny it. Her conscience, bothersome for once, wouldn't let her. It was true. "Nothing's like it used to be," she said, close to tears. "It used to be so friendly in the woodland. Now there are traps and snares everywhere."

Since Vicky was Vicky, the feeling of defeat did not last long. It is far easier to say or do a wrong thing, than to apologize for it, but she gritted her teeth and forced herself to do exactly that.

Housekeeper Amy, who loathed the countryside but didn't allow that to sour her good nature, gave the excuse, by making Beth Hewitt a bowl of broth. "Eating for two, poor love, and sickly with it," she said. "This'll do her a power of good."

Vicky asked to deliver the broth. That way, she could see Beth and say sorry to Ted Hewitt.

It went off quite well, in the end. Ted Hewitt glared at Vicky when he walked into the keeper's cottage and found her chatting to Beth. But he forgot his pride, once he knew why she was there. The strain of keeping his job made him bad-tempered – he knew that. "Perhaps I've been a bit hasty," he admitted to Vicky.

Conscience soothed, Vicky began to feel good again. Just then, Beth Hewitt groaned and almost fell.

"Lend a hand, Missie," Hewitt snapped, and they managed to lay Beth on a bed in the corner. A moment before Beth had been tired and pale, now, feverish, gasping with pain, she gripped her husband's hand and wailed when he tried to pull free and fetch the doctor.

Vicky darted to the door. "Don't worry, I'll get him." Tucking up her dress she pelted through the garden and out into the Eddington estate. She had come the long way, by the public road. But the ban was lifted, surely. Anyway, Hewitt wanted her father brought by the quickest route.

Running hard, Vicky wished she had been able to ride Black Beauty to the cottage. Then she could have gone like the wind, and . . .

Vicky never knew what happened next. The wire snare, running between two trees, noosed her ankle, threw her down, and knocked all the breath from her body.

She came round soon enough, tried to get up, and was pulled down with pain biting and throbbing in her leg. The wire loop had cut deeply into the soft leather of her ankle boot. Nails breaking, fingers bleeding, she tore and pulled at the thing.

Panic made Vicky clumsy. The pain didn't matter, but if she was trapped too long, Beth Hewitt might die. She was lying back there in the cottage, trapped and helpless – just like Vicky.

"Help, help me, I'm trapped. Somebody, please help." She had to get free, to fetch her father. But the wire bit tighter as she struggled with it, until she slumped back, frantic with worry but exhausted and beaten.

And then she heard it. A whinny, repeated from time to time, its tone a call and a question. The thudding of hooves on turf.

And there he was in the clearing, ebony hide gleaming, magical and unexpected and wonderful. Black Beauty snuffled at her cheek, as he did when seeking sugar. "Help me, Beauty. The wire, can you pull it out?"

There was a little slack running from her ankle to the nearest tree. Vicky lifted the wire and shook it, desperately.

Black Beauty stood still, looking at the wire.

Abruptly, he tossed his head, wheeled, and trotted back along the path. Watery lights showed the play of muscles as he moved – but for once, Vicky found no enchantment in the sight. Tears scalding, she threw herself down. The pain in her ankle nagged, but was drowned by the far greater misery of being deserted.

Within minutes, Vicky was bitterly ashamed of herself. That was when her father appeared, led by Black Beauty, to cut her free.

Dr. Gordon bit his lip as he unlaced Vicky's boot and saw the red weal on her skin. A shout made him look up. Ted Hewitt was lumbering down the path.

Vicky roused herself. "Father, Beth Hewitt – she needs you."

The gamekeeper was closer, now. "What're you doing, man?" he raged at Dr. Gordon. "My wife's dying, and you . . ." His words tailed away. He took in the whole picture: the snare, Vicky, an hour or more wasted. "Oh, no!" he groaned.

Dr. Gordon wasted no time on "I-told-you-so-ing". He helped his daughter over to Black Beauty. "I'm sorry, my dear, but if you ride carefully, you can bear the pain. Find Amy and tell her to meet me at Hewitt's cottage. She'll know what to bring."

Later, Kevin told Vicky what she had always told him – Black Beauty was a truly remarkable horse. First, to guess Vicky's plight, leap the paddock fence, and find her. Then, to return to York Cottage, frighten Amy into near-hysterics by following her around the kitchen garden, and then practically drag Dr. Gordon back to Vicky.

Saving Vicky from a long, painful wait was the least of Black Beauty's victories. The main one was in saving Beth Hewitt's life. Dr. Gordon had arrived just in time to deliver the baby and bring its mother back from the brink of death.

There came a certain day when Miss Vicky Gordon – once again an honoured visitor, free of the whole of the Eddington estate – rode over to see Beth Hewitt and the baby.

Black Beauty whinnied sharply as they passed the hut behind the cottage. Ted Hewitt was coming out, a tangled mass of wires and twine in his arms: perhaps two dozen snares. He added them to a heap of traps on top of the rubbish heap.

"That's the last of the ones from the paths," he said. He looked younger, less worried, now that his wife and child were safe. Vicky, sheepishly, wondered how she could have thought him such a brute.

"I'll have to leave some in the woodland, Missie. Vermin eat the young pheasants, and if Lord Eddington don't have a few brace of *them* to blaze away at, it's the end of my job," he explained. Vicky nodded, reluctantly. He was right, but the world could be cruel.

Hewitt rubbed his chin. "I'll look at the woodland snares every day. I've shaken your father by the hand, and I'll not break my word to his kin, Missie. Nothing caught in those snares will suffer too much, I promise."

Ted Hewitt looked from Vicky to Black Beauty arching his neck as though knowing of the debt he was owed. They made a fine sight, girl and horse together, thought Hewitt.

He raised a hand in full-hearted salute. "It's the least I can do."

Vicky, Dr Gordon, Black Beauty, Kevin, Amy

'Brother and sister ran across the grass'

Amy and Dr Gordon

Kevin and Vicky

'It was Samson with a much older man strapped into a wheelchair'

‘He is black and he is certainly very beautiful’

'A quarter of an hour later, Vicky was riding Black Beauty around the paddock'

Left: 'You're barred from this estate . . . keep out, young lady!'
Right: 'Nothing's like it used to be'

'Vicky never knew what happened next'

'That was when her father appeared'

'They made a fine sight together'

'Kevin couldn't get a word in'

'Vicky and Black Beauty followed'

'The one and only, Andy, the Clown on Horseback'

Left: 'Vicky nodded, miserable and impatient'
Right: 'Vicky and Kevin were twins . . .'

'We've all won'

'Hello, Susie. Come to visit us?'

Left:'You mustn't believe everything you hear'
Right:'Vicky hurled the grooming brush at Kevin's head, but felt no better'

Left: 'Willie Davidson didn't think so'
Right: 'Fox the groom fetched a package from the inn'

'Black Beauty would dip his head to listen when Vicky spoke to him in a certain way'

CLOWN ON HORSEBACK

Kevin was puzzled. He just knew he had seen the dancing clown. After all, it wasn't something he could have imagined.

It wasn't a dream. Not in the middle of the morning – he pinched himself just to make sure. It certainly wasn't a mirage. They only happened in the hot Sahara desert, not here in the old wood only a half mile from home.

No, he had seen him all right. He had been walking in the woods, as he often did. He liked to be by himself, to get away from Vicky who could talk of nothing but horses, and away from bossy old Amy who always found boring jobs for him to do about the house.

So most mornings Kevin stole away for an hour or so. He enjoyed exploring the woods and thinking what it must have been like in the olden days when the great trees covered all England and the ancient Britons held secret ceremonies in the forest glades.

He had been startled by a sound. A sort of

cackling, laughing sound. Then, through the trees he saw him. A tall thin man in a battered top hat and a patched tail-coat. His face was quite white, and for a nose he had a great red blob, like an over-ripe tomato.

He certainly looked like a clown. He even had those huge, ridiculous broken-toed boots that Kevin had seen in pictures of the circus.

The clown was performing a kind of dance, his big outsize boots flapping about on the old dead leaves. The clown must have been singing to himself, although all that Kevin could hear was that cackling laugh every now and again.

Soon the dance was over and apparently from nowhere three stools appeared by the clown's feet. He placed one stool on top of the other and then, with another cackling laugh, attempted to leap up and do a hand-stand on the topmost stool.

As he did so, the stools and the clown collapsed in a heap on the leaves. Now it was Kevin's turn to laugh. He couldn't help himself, it looked so funny, although possibly the poor clown had hurt himself in the fall.

At the sound of Kevin's laughter the clown jumped to his feet. In spite of his funny painted face there was an anger, a menace in his gesture.

Kevin darted behind a tree. He hid, not daring to breathe for what seemed ages. Then cautiously he looked out. The clown had gone. So had the stools. There was not a trace of him.

At lunch Kevin tried to tell his father about the strange disappearing clown. But Vicky who had spent the morning with Black Beauty at Mr. Collins' livery stables was full of some story about a new horse called Thunder that Mr. Collins was trying to break in.

Thunder was a very difficult horse. He had thrown Billy the stable boy and it had even taken Mr. Collins nearly an hour just to get the bridle on.

Kevin couldn't get a word in. When he did no one was listening.

"There he was," said Kevin taking advantage of a break in the conversation when Vicky had her mouth full, "There he was dancing all by himself."

"The horse?" asked Dr. Gordon mystified by this strange turn of the lunchtime conversation.

"No, the clown," said Kevin exasperated.

But by this time Vicky was back in the conversation talking about Thunder and Mr. Collins and Black Beauty and . . . and Kevin just gave up.

That afternoon he went back to the woods to find

his clown. He went again the next morning, and the morning after that. Nothing. Perhaps it was a dream after all.

Vicky meanwhile had been very busy at the livery stable. There had been some excitement when Thunder threw Mr. Collins and bolted off out of the paddock into a field.

Luckily Black Beauty had been there and had headed off the runaway horse before any damage had been done. Mr. Collins had said the horse was unmanageable, he had been ill-treated by a previous owner.

Vicky remembered the same had been true of Black Beauty, but love and patience had helped win back his confidence in human beings.

Mr. Collins admitted that there was a certain trust between Thunder and Black Beauty. He said that if Vicky and Beauty could tame Thunder, perhaps he might let them keep the horse. It wasn't a firm promise, but Mr. Collins had said it and that was enough for Vicky.

All the excitement and the problems of training Thunder dominated life at York Cottage for the rest of the week. Kevin had almost forgotten about his mysterious clown.

Then one morning, during his customary walk in the woods, he was gazing up at a large oak tree where he thought he had seen a squirrel scramble, when suddenly standing before him was a man.

He was tall and thin wearing simple farm worker's clothes. Although his face wasn't painted and there was no red tomato on his nose Kevin recognized him instantly. He was the clown.

"Are you spying on me?" asked the man.

Kevin was startled, but not at all frightened. "No, sir," he said, "I'm sorry I laughed at you the other day. But you looked so funny, I couldn't help laughing. I meant no harm. Honestly, sir."

The man's face lit up. "You found me funny did you son? Did you really find me funny?" The man looked incredibly happy.

He told Kevin his name was Andy Walker and that he had lived all his life in the circus. When he had been a boy he had worked with the animals, even looking after the elephants and the lions.

But as he got older he had to do other jobs. He had tried walking the highwire, but he had no head for heights. He had tried a job as Strong Man, but he was too skinny and anyway he couldn't lift the heavy weights.

Finally he joined the clowns. But that, too, was a disaster. Nobody ever laughed. Now he was to be turned out of the circus, unless, of course, he could improve his act. That's why he had been in the wood, practising to be a clown. The problem was that he didn't have an audience. He couldn't tell if he was funny or not.

Kevin thought that Andy Walker was really a very nice man. Here was a chance to see a clown at work without having to pay. Kevin volunteered – he would be the audience, a special audience of one.

It sounded so easy. But it wasn't. For Andy Walker was a very unfunny, inferior clown indeed.

As Dr. Gordon said to Amy Carter, both the children had found themselves a lost cause. Vicky up early each morning to train Thunder the unmanageable horse, and Kevin with his clown who could never make anyone laugh.

Kevin tried everything. He suggested that Andy attempted to juggle with a couple of eggs he had smuggled out of Amy's kitchen. That was a disaster. Within seconds the eggs ended up as a sort of omelet on Andy's boots.

Another day Andy announced he had a mime act. He sat on a stool and pretended to milk an imaginary cow. It was just as well he had told Kevin what he was doing, for the lad would never have guessed. It didn't look as if he was milking a cow, it didn't look like anything in particular. And it wasn't really very funny.

Vicky meanwhile had had little success with Thunder. By much trial and error she discovered the horse quite enjoyed trotting by the side of Black Beauty, but he would not allow anyone to ride him. And it was impossible to put a saddle on him.

One morning Vicky riding Black Beauty took Thunder on a leading rein for a canter across the fields. She thought that if they got away from the atmosphere of the stables Thunder might be more willing to be saddled up and ridden. She was wrong.

They had barely been out half an hour when Thunder broke free and raced away. Vicky and Black Beauty followed but Thunder galloped like a mad thing, jumping ditches, smashing through hedgerows, leaving a trail of destruction behind him.

A flock of sheep scurried noisily out of his way and only the cows seemed to ignore the chase, peacefully chewing the cud. Thunder seemed to have no sense of direction. He just ran wild, though it did look as if he might have been making for the wood.

In the wood Andy was showing Kevin his new clown's make-up. At least he said it was a clown's make-up, Kevin thought it looked more like a skull. It was quite horrible: dead white, black eyes, black nose and mouth. It would never make children laugh, give them nightmares more likely.

Andy was trying to wipe the grease-paint off his

face when they heard the horses. They ran out of the wood and saw Thunder racing toward them.

"Look out!" screamed Kevin as Andy ran right in front of the runaway horse but Andy grabbed at the reins as Thunder galloped by and shouted something.

It was amazing. Thunder stopped. He stood breathing heavily, with Andy by his side whispering in his ear.

At that moment Vicky appeared on Black Beauty. "Is everything all right?" she asked.

Andy nodded. "I understand animals," he said, and then he jumped up on Thunder and rode him bareback across the field. Vicky watched in amazement, but in Kevin's mind an idea was forming.

It had been planned for several months, a children's party organized by Dr. Gordon in the garden of York Cottage. All the farm workers' children from the village had been invited. Amy had spent days cooking cream cakes and making pastry.

It was near the end of the party, when almost all the lemonade had been drunk, that Kevin stood up on the table to make an announcement.

"Ladies and Gentlemen," he shouted, "I present to

you for the first time on any stage . . . before your very eyes . . . the one and only, Andy, the Clown on Horseback!"

Out of the stables stepped Thunder with Andy, wearing his battered top hat and red nose, riding him bare-back. The children shrieked with delight as the clown and the horse went through their tricks.

However clumsy Andy had been on the ground, he was as nimble as anything on horseback. Even Kevin was amazed.

More amazed was Mr. Collins who watched the show from Amy's kitchen. He told Vicky he had promised her Thunder if the horse could be trained and now she could have him.

"Oh, no," said Vicky. "It wasn't me that did it. It was Andy."

Mr. Collins thought for a while. "In that case," he said, "it is Andy who shall have him."

And that is how the circus found two new stars, Andy Walker and Thunder, topping the bill: the Clown on Horseback.

HORSE THIEVES

Henry Bullivant's nickname was "Gunpowder" because he liked blowing things up. In fact, he loved explosions, the bigger the better.

He was the man in charge of building a new railway line near Five Oaks village. The Great Western Railway company actually *paid* him to blow holes through rocks and hills, so that trains could take short-cuts.

Mr. Bullivant, a great friend of Dr. Gordon, was a happy man.

He looked it that morning, grinning down at Vicky and Kevin. They were near – but not too near – Marne Hill, a local landmark. It looked sleepy and unchanging did Marne Hill.

"Gunpowder" Bullivant meant to change all that. "Cheer up, Vicky," he said. "I'll just blast this cutting through the hill, and then we'll get your precious horse back. My rascals are bound to have put him among our nags. Hide a leaf in a forest, eh?"

Vicky nodded, miserable and impatient. Put Black Beauty in a "forest" of a million horses, and she'd pick him out.

Only an hour before, she and Kevin had found Black Beauty's stable empty, with no sign of the horse. Vicky willed herself to be calm. Things could be a lot worse. And she had to admit that Kevin had found the vital clue. Down in the straw lay a clasp knife, with a name, M. SULLIVAN, clearly engraved on the handle.

Kevin had brains, where his sister had spirit. "Those two men we saw in the lane yesterday," he reminded her. "Those Irish navvies who couldn't stop looking at Black Beauty. Well, one of them was using this knife to hack a bit of wood. Don't you see, you goose? Now we *know* who's stolen Black Beauty, we're bound to get him back."

This was good news. Mr. Bullivant's word was law to the army of navvies, the workmen building the railway. He'd make them all down tools and search for Black Beauty. The children had no doubt where "M. Sullivan" would hide him – somewhere among the hundreds of working horses.

The railway builders had riding horses for surveyors and foremen, shire horses to pull the big wagons carrying sleepers and rails and ballast, and tough little ponies to haul earth away as the navvies pick-and-shovelled it aside.

Finding Black Beauty was only a matter of time. But what Vicky and Kevin didn't know was that there was hardly any time left.

So here they were, Mr. Bullivant, Kevin, and Vicky, waiting to see Marne Hill blown sky high. Vicky hated loud noises, but she wished "Gunpowder" Bullivant would get on with this one, so that Black Beauty could be found.

One of the building foremen, hearing about Black Beauty, gave Vicky a wink. "I've got a hundred men around here, to warn people away from the explosion, Missie," he said. "It's certain your horse can't be anywhere near Marne Hill."

The foreman was wrong. Black Beauty *was* "near Marne Hill". Right inside it, to be exact. Michael Sullivan, owner of that lost knife, and his mate Jim Hooley, had hidden him in a cave there.

Black Beauty didn't look like Vicky's pride and joy any more. An old sack was tied round his head, to blind and silence him. Jim and Michael had smeared oil and soot on his lighter markings, to change them. His usually sleek hide was matted with mud and dust and sweat.

Meanwhile Jim and Michael had sneaked back to York Cottage, hoping to find Michael's knife before it gave them away. Though they were too late, they heard Mr. Bullivant saying to Dr. Gordon; "I've got permission at last. I shall blow the cutting through Marne Hill first thing this morning. The gunpowder's ready."

Jim and Michael, hiding and listening, felt as if *they'd* had gunpowder exploded under them. They might be thieves, but they weren't needlessly cruel. Prison or not, they wouldn't let Black Beauty be blown to smithereens. As Mr. Bullivant rode off, they told Dr. Gordon what they'd done – and why the explosion must be delayed.

Everybody was making for Marne Hill that morning. Mr. "Gunpowder" Bullivant, to blow it up. Vicky and Kevin, going there to see him, and ask his help in recovering Black Beauty. Finally, the two horse-thieves and Dr. Gordon, running like mad to stop the explosions.

At the hill, Mr. Bullivant smacked his lips, cleared his throat, and gave his very favourite order. "Light the fuses!" He picked up his telescope. "All be over in, oh, a minute or less."

Then he passed the telescope to Kevin who gasped as he put the tube to his eye, and saw the hillside jump closer. He could see Jim Hooley scrambling down the hill, right into the area holding the gunpowder, Mr. Bullivant and the foreman spotted him too. They bellowed and danced and waved their arms. "Get back, you fool, get back!"

Vicky took the telescope in time to see Jim Hooley vanish into the solid hillside, just like a ghost walking through a wall. "He ... just ... disappeared," she gasped.

Kevin and Vicky were twins. Though they argued and had different natures, danger always drew them together. In that instant, somehow, their brains combined into one unit.

Kevin dealt with the disappearing bit. "A cave," he guessed, recalling village tales about one being somewhere in Marne Hill.

Vicky asked why Jim Hooley should risk his life to get to a cave. Caves were used to hide treasure and robber's plunder and – "Beauty!" she cried out.

As Kevin and Vicky pelted toward's the cave, Jim was ripping the sack off Black Beauty's head before leading him out.

Mr. Bullivant knew it was too late to stop the fuses. Chasing the children, he knocked them flat. Instantly, the ground heaved, there was a not-very-loud bang, and a few pebbles and twigs came bouncing down on their backs.

Kevin felt quite cheated. Call that an explosion, he thought. I could do better with a firework! Vicky, naturally, didn't mind. Back on her feet, she could hear a distant whinny. "He's alive, Black Beauty's alive," she shouted.

Her face lit up. "Of course he is," Kevin answered. But Vicky was staring at Mr. Bullivant, who held her back and gazed at his watch. "Fifteen seconds . . ." he announced.

There were two explosions due that morning. One to clear a little earth away, then what Mr. Bullivant called, "The big feller, the real crack-of-doom affair."

Vicky broke away from him. She went forward, thinking fast – faster than the flame on the fuse.

Black Beauty's neighing, and the clash of his hoofs, came echoing from the cave, telling Vicky that he was in a blind panic, fighting Jim Hooley instead of running to safety.

She had to pack everything into one word. Everything to calm him, make him think, make him win the race against the gunpowder. But what word? Vicky took a deep breath.

Making her voice normal, almost casual, she called out: "Beauty!" A call to remind him of open fields, love, and kindness.

Black Beauty, only seconds away from death, caught the sound and understood the message. He snorted once, wheeling to face the mouth of the cave. Jim Hooley leaped on his back, urging him forward.

Black Beauty didn't mind the strange weight and

feel of the rider. His mistress was calling for him, that was good enough . . .

Outside, there was a roar like a clap of thunder, battering the surrounding country. Kevin and Vicky were knocked flat again – Kevin always swore, afterwards, that he saw a whole oak tree, roots and all, flying at least fifty feet into the air. A huge new valley was carved in the green hill, showing through a cloud of dust which dimmed the sun.

Vicky was deafened. Frantically she rubbed the dust out of her eyes. And there, in the heart of the dust cloud, was Black Beauty. Neck stretched, eyes only for her, he was galloping straight towards her.

Mr. Bullivant, for once, wasn't interested in his latest explosion. He hugged Vicky and pounded Kevin on the back. "He got away, he got away! Magnificent animal, simply magnificent. Won his race, all right – and few living things beat gunpowder."

Vicky, through tears of happiness, watched Black Beauty slow to a walk, while Jim Hooley slipped off his back and tried to look innocent. And then she shook her head.

"He didn't win the race. Not on his own, anyway. We all did – even those brutes who stole him. We've all won, Mr. Bullivant, we've all won!"

THE HORSEMEN

Ask young Vicky Gordon to imagine the worst event in the world and her answer would come back in a flash.

"Losing Black Beauty."

So the brief meeting with Susan Oldfield made Vicky go white, while her heart jumped and fluttered. It was like walking into a nightmare, eyes wide open, on a sunny day.

Vicky came across the stableyard having spent a long, hard grooming session with Black Beauty. Now he gleamed like watered silk. The light shining through the half-door of the stable made fascinating patterns on his sides.

But Vicky had heard a carriage pull up outside York Cottage, and wanted to see who had arrived.

"Hello, Susie. Come to visit us?" Vicky smiled up at the pretty girl fidgeting impatiently in the open carriage. Most girls envied Susan Oldfield, spoiled only daughter of the richest man in the district, but Vicky always felt a bit sorry for her. Susan might have more dresses, and trinkets, at the early age of 17, than many grown women. But she was bored, always greedy but never quite sure what she wanted.

Susan stared down at the bright-faced Vicky. "We've come to buy the horse," she drawled. And when the other girl looked puzzled, Susan explained, "Black Beauty, of course."

Vicky gulped, feeling giddy and short of breath. *No, no!* "You're joking," she whispered, hoping to see the older girl burst into mocking laughter.

But Susan merely smiled; a well-fed-cat smile, teasing and confident. "You'll find it's no joke. Father's inside, buying him now."

An angry, fearful little whirlwind burst into Dr. James Gordon's study before Susan Oldfield finished the words. Vicky flung herself at her father. "You're not selling Black Beauty. You can't!"

Dr. Gordon was startled. "Of course not, Vicky."

Mr. Oldfield liked to get his own way. And the doctor had turned him down, even when he had offered one hundred and fifty guineas – a small fortune – for Black Beauty. But now, even though Susan would fly into a tantrum at the news, Mr. Oldfield was glad that he had failed to buy the horse.

He smiled at Vicky. "Don't worry, lass. Black Beauty's still yours."

In the study, Dr. Gordon was shaking his head, as colour crept back into his daughter's cheeks. "Vicky, Vicky. Black Beauty has no match when it comes to jumping walls and fences. But you, child – you're a champion at jumping to conclusions."

Putting his hands on her shoulders, Dr. Gordon added, "You mustn't believe everything you hear, sweetheart. Find out for yourself, eh?"

Vicky wasn't listening. Black Beauty was safe! *I'll never be parted from you, never,* she thought.

Vicky would have been less relieved if she had overheard a conversation between Susan Oldfield, Mr. Oldfield, and their groom, Fox, a few hours before.

The threesome, in their carriage, had been watching Vicky riding Black Beauty across a field near York Cottage. Susan, boredom swept away for once, stood up in the carriage, hands twisting. "He's beautiful, I must have him. I must. Buy him for me, father, you can buy anything."

Mr. Oldfield chuckled and slapped his pocket. "I dare say."

Fox, the groom, wasn't so sure. Fox lived up to his name – sly, knowing, ready for devilment. One of the things he knew was that Black Beauty was more than a horse, he was a member of the Gordon family.

"They won't sell, Miss. Not without a lot of persuasion," he warned. Fox often made money on the sly, slipped to him by Susan Oldfield, for making her whims come true. This was his way of telling her that he wanted an even bigger bribe than usual.

"They've got to sell," the girl snapped. "I'd give anything, anything!" And Fox clicked his tongue to the horses and flicked the reins to move them on.

Vicky missed all that, but somebody heard. Down in a dip, out of sight of the carriage, was a battered but gaudy-painted caravan. It belonged to McPhee, the tinker.

McPhee had forgotten more about horses than many a man ever learns. He also stole them, from time to time. He was one of "The Travelling People", hating to stay in one place for long. But he was rooted to Five Oaks for the moment, while Dr. Gordon cured his youngest son of a nasty bout of coughing.

On the Sunday after the false alarm over Black Beauty's sale, the Gordons came back from church to hear a bucket rattle in the stable. Vicky, still rather nervous about her precious Black Beauty, dashed to investigate. She was sure somebody had been prowling about.

"It could have been the tinker," she muttered, suspiciously. "Stealing food for his horse. The villagers say all tinkers are thieves."

Dr. Gordon frowned at her. "Tinkers are like everyone else, some are good, some bad," he said sharply. "McPhee is a decent fellow, very grateful about my treating his little boy."

Vicky was unconvinced, even when she went to McPhee's camp with her father. The tinker denied going to York Cottage.

Remembering the scene with the Oldfields, and Fox, he tried to warn her, though. "Other people are interested in your horse, Miss," he hinted. Vicky brushed the suggestion aside. The Susan Oldfield business was over . . . she thought.

The next few days brought Vicky nightmares of another kind. Black Beauty threatened to go out of control. He shied, he bucked, he refused to go into perfectly innocent field-gates, he was frightened by the simplest stretch of road.

"So much for your fine talk about being closer to him than anyone else in the world," her brother Kevin pointed out. "He's only a horse, Vicky. A wonderful horse – but only a horse."

Vicky hurled the grooming brush at Kevin's head, but felt no better. Housekeeper Amy nagged her for not eating her meals. Shadows appeared under the girl's eyes.

She had always been so close to Black Beauty. He seemed to understand her words, and replied in his own language: a neigh, a whinny, rolling his eyes or flicking his ears. Once she had longed to learn the lauguage – somebody must know it – but now, even the simplest orders went wrong.

"I just don't seem able to handle him any more," she said, miserably. "Is it my fault?" she appealed to her father.

Willie Davidson, the blacksmith, didn't think so. A bent and lined old veteran, there was little he did not know about his trade. His old cap looked like a hot-cross bun – he was always snatching it off to pick up hot bits of iron, scorching the cloth.

Vicky took Black Beauty to him for a new shoe and poured out her worries. How Black Beauty took fright at nothing, and forgot their friendship to fight and shy away from her.

"I think you've got an enemy," old Willie told her, mysteriously. "Maybe I should take a look at that stable of yours."

They returned to York Cottage, and as had become usual over the past week, Black Beauty made a great fuss about going into the stable. The blacksmith hobbled up to the door, sniffing hard. Suddenly he cackled with laughter and slapped his thigh. "Got it," he shouted.

To Vicky's amazement, he grabbed a stable lantern, tipped out some of the oil and rubbed it up and down the doorposts. "Walk him in now, Miss Vic," he suggested.

Black Beauty went straight in, as of old. "How did you do it?" Vicky cried, clapping her hands.

"Horse has a better nose than you have, Miss Vic. He caught the smell of something put on that door, to make you think he was acting up. But I can't tell you anything more. Let's just say I took an oath, once." And Willie Davidson stumped away.

If Vicky thought their troubles were over, she was mistaken. Next day, she was riding Black Beauty down a quiet lane, when he began fighting the bit. The next five minutes seemed to last for years. Black Beauty danced, reared, arched his back, foam flying from his mouth. Without warning, for the first time in their partnership, Vicky was frightened. All her skill went for nothing. Black Beauty was in the grip of a maddening ghost, forgetting the girl in the saddle. Branches lashed her face, her arms ached and lost their power.

It had to happen – Vicky went flying, heading for a nasty heap of jagged stones at the side of the lane. Luckily, Willie Davidson was near and had seen the situation building up. Dropping his tool bag, he ran up as fast as he could, catching Vicky so that they both fell in an untidy sprawl on long grass to one side of the stones.

Once they were on their feet, Willie went straight to Black Beauty, calmed him with a couple of muttered words, and unbuckled the girth. He spoke angrily, as he pulled the heavy strap from under the saddle.

"This has got irritant put on it. Stuff that's meant for inflamed joints. Only gets to work when the horse warms up, then drives the poor beast frantic. And look out, the poor rider!"

Willie started to say something else, then stopped and went red. Vicky knew what he had in mind. If she had hurt herself, Black Beauty would have been sold as a vicious animal unfit for anything but the toughest, most brutal rider. She shivered realizing that Dr. Gordon wouldn't sell a killer horse. He would have had Black Beauty shot. More in sorrow than in anger, but he would have done it. Because that seemed the only answer.

"Who would do a thing like this?" she sobbed.

"Whoever it was knows the secrets of The Horsemen's Society," Willie growled. "It's an old secret society with ways of controlling horses with herbs and suchlike things. But this is misusing the craft, turning it to evil, and that's the crowning crime."

Vicky frowned. "Could a tinker be a member?" She was thinking of McPhee, with his bright, sharp eyes gloating at Black Beauty whenever they rode past.

Willie Davidson had thoughts of his own. "You walk Beauty home, Miss Vic. I'll give some thought to how we can catch this fellow out – whoever he is."

Vicky had to be satisfied with that. Her father flatly refused to send McPhee packing, without proof that he was behind the plot. "McPhee's little boy needs rest. And anyway, I'm sure McPhee wouldn't play such tricks, even if he *did* want to get the horse cheap and sell dear, as he would say."

A day or so later, Willie Davidson called for Vicky. Though his hair was grey and he was a long way past 60 he looked like a mischievous schoolboy.

He led her to a hiding place near a country inn. "I've done my work," Willie whispered. "Now we shall see what we shall see." His work-worn body was shaking with laughter and excitement.

Vicky spotted the Oldfield carriage. Susan lounged on the cushions, while Fox the groom fetched a package from the inn. Susan was eager to go, and Fox leaped up to the driving seat and shook the reins.

The horse wouldn't move. Fox shouted, encouraged, flicked the whip, cracked it, leaned forward to slap the horse's rump. But it was like dealing with a wooden animal, or one turned to stone.

"You did that," Vicky blurted out. Willie put a finger to his lips, and winked.

"That stuff on the doorpost, it can go on a horse's legs as well, Miss Vic. If the smell comes from ahead of him, on his forelegs, he won't go forward. Not for anything."

They heard Susan whine, "Oh, do get on, Fox. Why can't we go?"

Fox was wondering the same thing. He jumped down, ran his hand along the horse's foreleg, and sniffed his palm. All of a sudden he didn't look so cocky. He pulled a flat bottle from his pocket, poured something colourless into his palm, and rubbed the stuff around the carriage horse's mouth and nostrils.

"Gin," Willie explained, still whispering. "The horse'll go now, Miss Vic. Can't smell nothing but the gin." Fox snapped the reins and the carriage moved out of the inn yard, onto the highway.

Willie straightened up from the hiding place, with a groan for his back, and spread his arms to stop the carriage. Vicky slid down the bank after him.

"I see you know the Horsemen's secrets, Mr. Fox," said Willie. Fox's face was a picture of guilt. As for

Susan Oldfield, she looked just as guilty, and ashamed at being caught. "Fox, you idiot! You've been tricked," she screamed. "Drive on, drive *on*!" She couldn't get away fast enough.

Fox, egged on by Susan, had been using secret herbs and medicines to make Black Beauty seem a rogue horse. Mr. Oldfield, Susan's father, was furious with the pair of them, and promised to give his daughter a lesson she would not forget in a hurry.

Vicky didn't care. She was not vindictive, and was too overjoyed at Black Beauty's return to normal, to want revenge.

"I always said I couldn't bear to lose you," she whispered to Black Beauty. "And when it seemed that I *could* lose you – the real you – even though you were here all the time . . . oh, it was terrible."

Black Beauty whinnied, nuzzling her hair. Vicky was not sure whether he was telling her that he had hated disobeying her, too, or simply that he would always be her friend. "If only I knew exactly what you were saying," she thought.

Dr. Gordon told her that Mr. Oldfield had called to apologize. "And you owe somebody an apology, too," he reminded her.

"Yes, I know." Vicky patted Black Beauty's nose.

"I suspected McPhee, just because he was a tinker. Say it, Black Beauty – shame on me!"

McPhee was making willow baskets in the shade of his caravan, when Vicky called. He guessed her errand from her face. "So you found out who it was, playing tricks on your horse," he greeted her.

"Yes, and I'm very sorry for thinking that you . . ."

McPhee grinned and shook his head. His eyes twinkled, and Vicky gasped. "Are . . . are *you* a member of the Horsemen's Society?" Somehow she knew that he suspected Fox's tricks, all along. If he was one of The Horsemen, he would know the tricks being used. "Are you?" she persisted.

McPhee hesitated, face serious for once. Then he nodded.

Vicky saw her chance. Maybe she could find out if horses did have a language of their own. "Will you tell me about The Society?" she pleaded.

"I'm not allowed to," said McPhee. "But after what your father has done for my little boy, I'll tell you all I know about horses . . . Except the Horsemen's secrets."

They had a long talk, McPhee hammering his wisdom home with rhymes and old proverbs. Vicky went home in thoughtful mood, seeing Black Beauty with new eyes and fresh knowledge.

More than ever she was certain that Black Beauty was held to her by a special link. And she took to talking to him last thing at night, in the oddest way. As soon as Kevin came near, she would stop, pretending to be singing or talking to herself.

Kevin jeered at her, of course. "Fancy swallowing McPhee's blarney," he scoffed.

But Black Beauty would dip his head and listen, when Vicky spoke to him in a certain way. And when Kevin poked fun, she did not flare up and chase him, in the old way.

Vicky just smiled, rather pityingly. And Kevin, to his own fury, could have sworn that Black Beauty smiled with her . . .